SIMON SIMONIAN

THE LAST SCION OF THE MOUNTAINEERS
(ON THE OCCASION OF THE 30TH ANNIVERSARY OF HIS DEATH)

LEVON SHAROYAN
TRANSLATED BY VAHE H. APELIAN, Ph.D.

Contents

Preface

A Labor of Love

This book is a labor of love.

It started last year when, amidst war and destruction in Aleppo, Levon Sharoyan wrote a very personal monograph about the eminent man of letters, Simon Simonian. He published it in installments first on his Facebook page, later on in a more expanded version in "Kantsasar" Weekly, the official newsletter of the Prelacy of the Armenian Apostolic Church in Aleppo, and also almost simultaneously, in "Aztag" Daily in Lebanon and in "Nor Haratch", a tri-weekly, in Paris.

Levon's monograph was his tribute to his elder compatriot. Levon's grandfather, much like Simon Simonian's father, hailed from Sassoun, a mountainous region in Western Armenia, and was depicted among the stories Simon Simonian wrote about the struggles of the Sassountsi mountaineers on the plains of Aleppo, in Syria, far from their native mountain top villages.

The monograph, which since then has been published as a book in Armenia, made for a fascinating reading. I thought that it would be unfair for those who do not read Armenian to remain deprived of such a reading. Consequently, I asked Levon's permission to have it translated into English. He readily gave it.

I then contacted Sassoun Simonian, Simon Simonian's youngest son, to convey him my intention. It turned out that Sassoun had also thought of the same. Not only that, coincidentally, having read my published translation of one of Simon Simonian's most endearing stories titled "He Was Different", he had me in mind for the task for a fee. Naturally, I categorically declined the monetary offer while appreciating his trust. Hence the draft of my translation of Levon Sharoyan's monograph came about. As to my translated story, it is included in this book as an addendum. It was also published in Keghart.com. Its title in Armenian is "An Ourish Er".

Upon Sassoun's recommendation, I sent a copy of my

draft to his niece Maria-Eleni Simonian, who read the monograph and pointed out typos and offered suggestions. At the end of her review she added the following note:

"Dear Mr. Apelian,

It was a great pleasure to be able to read and learn more about my grandfather. It is one of my aspirations to learn Armenian and read his work to get a small picture of who he was. I believe you brought justice to your endeavor. Thank you for your time and contribution.

Kind regards,
Maria-Eleni Simonian"

Her note validated the undertaking of this task. I also sent a copy of my manuscript to my maternal cousin Jack Chelebian M.D. Jack graciously and ably corrected and edited my draft manuscript by painstakingly comparing it line by line to the original text. Jack spent no less time than I did in finalizing the translation. I can certainly attest that this translated piece is true to the original.

It is also fair to note here that Simon Simonian and Jack's father, Dr. Antranig (Chelebian) Chalabian, were friends. It was Simon Simonian who made possible the publication of Henry Glockler's memoir titled "Interned in Turkey 1914-1918" for a nominal fee the author had sent to Dr. Antranig Chalabian to help him publish his memoirs that Chalabian had edited.

Sassoun Simonian also read the draft translation and offered valuable suggestions in presenting the titles of Simon Simonian's books as well as the personal names and retrieved from his father's archive, located in Antelias, Lebanon, the many pictures that grace this book.

Transliteration is an inherent part of translations. There arises a challenging situation because Eastern Armenian and Western Armenian are not necessarily transliterated similarly. Whenever possible I resorted to the internet search engines to check on the common English transliteration of names in Western Armenian. The titles of the books that Simon Simonian wrote are transliterated and translated.

This will be the first book in English about the eminent man of letters, the late Simon Simonian. I pray that readers find the translation of Levon Sharoyan's book as enjoyable to read as I did the original.

Vahe H. Apelian, Ph.D.

1

Introduction

Simon Simonian

I borrowed the title of this book from an old article I wrote that was published in "Haratch", "Forward", Daily in Paris on July 13, 1986. I was a new contributor to the newspaper, a novice correspondent from Aleppo taking my hesitant steps onto the Armenian Diaspora press. Moved by the news of the eminent author's death, I had written the article in the immediate aftermath of Simon Simonian's death that had occurred on his birthday on March 24, 1986. Although the article was short and written in a single breath, it had covered an entire page.

To be honest, I need to confess that in those days I had not yet formulated a well-founded appreciation of Simonian's literary merit and of his many attributes. I had remained greatly impressed by the "Spurk", "Diaspora" Weekly he had published in Beirut. Apparently, my father was a subscriber to that paper. He had the foresightedness to preserve the issues. He had neatly folded and stacked them one on top of the other and bundled them in a few piles and had placed them in a leather bag, which was then stored in our attic.

I was still a school-age teenager when one day I discovered the issues when I stumbled upon the leather bag while rummaging in the attic. The many literary and cultural articles presented in the Weekly by a range of authors and by the editor of the Weekly, Simon Simonian, not only fascinated me but also carried me into a different world. Days and at times weeks on end, I would be engrossed reading the writings that would take me to a time that preceded me by 15 to 20 years. The other element that captivated me was the eloquence of the Armenian language with which the myriads of issues were explored. Perhaps, through reading these articles, I unconsciously polished my own literary language and laid the foundation of mastering my language and thought process.

Simon Simonian at the editor's desk
in his "Sevan" publishing & printing house

Thus I came to know of Simon Simonian through the "Spurk" Weekly. When I wrote the article in "Haratch" Daily, I had read a few of the stories in his book titled "Lernagannerou Verchaluyse", "The Twilight of the Mountaineers". Consequently, my impression of him was primarily distilled from my readings of his writings in the Weekly.

For the sake of history let me state that in those days, some thirty years ago, with a few literary minded friends, we paid a tribute to Simonian's literary legacy by organizing a public remembrance. The event took place on May 20, 1986, barely two months after his death. The event remains etched in the memory of those who organized the tribute.

2

Remembering
Simon Simonian and Aram Haigaz

I had graduated from the Karen Jeppe Jemaran a few months before our Simon Simonian and Aram Haigaz remembrance event. Even before I received my graduation diploma, representatives from the Hamazkayin Armenian Cultural & Educational Society had formally invited me to take part in the Society's Literary Committee.

It was at that time, March 1986, when we received the sad news of the passing away of the two eminent Diaspora authors, Aram Haigaz and Simon Simonian. The former had passed away in New York at the age of 86 and the latter in Beirut at the age of 72. The members of the Literary Committee, who were all graduates of the Jemaran, hastily decided to commemorate the deceased writers' literary legacies.

These two writers enjoyed a favorable reputation in the Aleppo Armenian community. The overwhelming majority of the students remembered Aram Haigaz because his literature was part of our curriculum. Simon Simonian was revered as a former member of the Aleppo Armenian community and had a large audience especially among the Sassountsis, his friends, and acquaintances in Aleppo.

Simon Simonian and Aram Haigaz
commemoration invitation card

We decided on a program, invited the speakers, and decided the date, the time and the location. We prepared and printed the flyers and the invitations, posted and distributed them all ourselves. The Hamazkayin "Nigol Aghpalian Hall", which is situated next to the Holy Forty Martyrs Cathedral, was filled to capacity when we started the program.

Hrach Kalsahakian (presently in Dubai), Rebecca Mavlian (presently in Australia) presented Aram Haigaz's literary contributions. Eugene Tanielian (presently in Armenia) and your humble servant presented Simon Simonian's literary contributions. The audience, not only commended the program, but former colleagues and friends of Simonian, came onto the stage on the spur of the moment, and gave their own testimonials. Mr. Pilibos Tertsagian, the principal of the Haigazian School, and a former colleague and Megerdich Megerdichian, a friend, and a compatriot gave moving eulogies about Simon Simonian.

We, as young members of Aleppo's Hamazkayin Armenian Educational & Cultural Society's Literary Group, who had organized the program, felt elated and proud of our achievement for the evening. That is how we stepped into our young adulthood thirty years ago.

Simon Simonian (on the left) and Pilibos Tertsagian with the boys'
section of the Haigazian National School 1945-1946 graduating
class in Aleppo, Syria

3

Armenian History Textbooks that Always Fascinated Me

Just recently, when I realized that it's the 30th anniversary of Simon Simonian's death, I went to my library and picked his famous multi-volume Armenian history textbooks and started perusing them all the while reminiscing about my old school days. On and off I have done the same in the past as well. I do that because I remain profoundly impressed by the mesmerizing content of the series and by the many black and white historical pictures. I reread chapters from here and there just to be amazed by the author's linguistic and narrative skills.

Many in the Diaspora remember these textbooks that became the standard history textbooks in the Armenian schools not only in Lebanon and Syria but also in Cyprus, Greece, the United States, Argentina, Jerusalem, and Ethiopia.

Who knows how many generations made their connections to their illustrious history through these textbooks? How many generations molded their identity as Armenians through these history textbooks? Countless are those who came to know of David of Sassoun, Lion Mher, Dragon fighting Vahakn, our legendary patriarch Haig, Ara the Beautiful, the pagan gods that brought the dead to life by licking their wounds, King Baruyr, Dikran the Great, Ardashes the Conqueror, the imprisoned King Arshag, Moushegh Mamigonian on his white horse, King Vramshabouh, Vartan who was killed in the battle of Avarayr and the Pakradouni Kings who built Ani. Roupen, Toros, Levon who established sovereignty on the Taurus Mountains, and all the other heroes of our history.

I was an elementary school student when my mother gifted me this sequel of Simonian's Armenian history textbooks that were bound in a single volume. From the very first page, I remained attached to the large volume. I would read the sequel page by page and would be moved looking at those mysterious pictures. I would remain fascinated by the bravery of the Armenian kings.

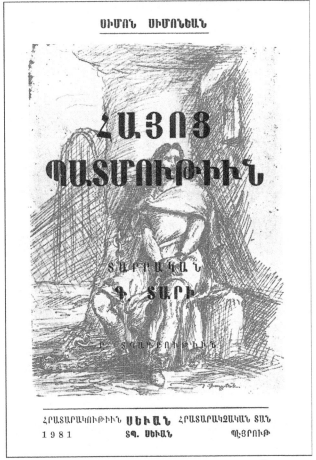

The 8th edition of the "Armenian History"
textbook for grade III

Simonian's writing style was captivating. It was not a cut and dry history that Simonian narrated. He inspired and reinforced his adolescent readers' Armenian identity.

In my formative years when I would not put down from my lap Simonian's history textbooks, I had no interest in him although his name was on the cover of the books. His name meant nothing to me. I was simply thankful for my mother for her thoughtful and precious gift.

At the very beginning of the first volume, Simon Simonian had placed a paragraph titled "The Reflection of the Armenian Student", like a covenant of faith. It reads:

> *"I am an Armenian. My fatherland, where my forefathers have lived and died is called Armenia. But I do not live in Armenia. I am away from it in exile.*
>
> *Above all, I will love my fatherland and I will not forget its name. I firmly believe that I will return there one day. To hasten that day, I will always read the history of my brave ancestors. I will love my church and my fatherland and I will feel proud to be called ARMENIAN.*

> *I have vowed to remain worthy to see*
> *Massis and Arakadz; Sipan and Nemrut;*
> *Puragn and Davros; Arax and Sevan;*
> *Etchmiadzin and Saint Garabed; Gars*
> *and Garin; Van and Mush."*

What a structure for students to be prepared for and introduced to Armenian history!

In writing his history textbooks, Simonian had adopted a very practical and helpful method. He narrated a historical event with a pleasant and in an easy to read language. He then listed key words, which might be unfamiliar to the students by listing them under a header titled "Explanatory Words" with an explanation for each. He listed eight to ten questions related to the narration under "Questionnaire" header. He then listed "Points for Elaboration" for the teacher to provide more details. At the end, he listed under "Sources", references that could help teachers and anyone else interested to expand his or her knowledge about Armenian history. For example, when he narrated the period of the Arab invasion of Armenia, he listed the following sources at the end of the chapter: Sepeos, historian Ghevont, Tovma Ardzrouni, as ancient Armenian historians, as well as books published in Venice and Vienna including a source in French.

Let us be mindful that Simon Simonian was barely 25 to 26 years old when he prepared his series of history textbooks.

4

Plagiarism of Simon Simonian's Armenian History Textbooks

"Plagiarism" is a word that is often used in literary circles. It is the sort of theft that takes place in the literary field. That is to say the loot, in this case, is not gold or money or valuable items; it is rather a written expression, sometimes sentences, at times paragraphs, and other times pages long. When a writer attempts to appropriate another writer's writing in full or in part as his or her own, that writer commits plagiarism. It's a condemnable act.

Personally, whenever I hear the word "plagiarism", I am reminded of Archbishop Yeghishe Derderian of the Patriarchate of Jerusalem who wrote under the pen name Yeghivart. In his younger days, he had plagiarized some of Hagop Oshagan's poems. Those stunning appropriations were exposed and condemned by the literary critic and author Boghos Snabian in 1951 in "Nayiri" Monthly, a literary magazine in Aleppo. Likewise, in the more distant past, the writings of Bishop Karekin Srvandsyants were plagiarized. In a book he published in 1884, titled "Hamov Hodov", implying on the lighter side, he noted that he was surprised to see some of his writings being published in newspapers by others. "I was surprised," he wrote, "but I kept quiet because the despicable act of literary theft was not new among us".

Simon Simonian's famous textbooks titled "Hayots Badmoutiun", "Armenian History", also were plagiarized.

Indeed, Armen Anoush-Marashlian (1907-1958), an intellect, a poet and a well-known prose-writer in Aleppo, who was also the principal of a school, beginning in 1953 started publishing a series of history textbooks similar to the ones Simon Simonian had first published beginning from 1939-41. Armen Anoush's history textbooks were reprinted a few times. Later it became evident that he had directly benefited from Simonian's textbooks, at times verbatim.

The first edition of the "Armenian History" textbook for grade I
printed in Aleppo in 1939.

Simon Simonian was very upset. He even prepared a study by comparing the two textbooks to defend against this encroachment. Later he decided against publishing his findings "to spare the reputations of national and pedagogical figures", in his own words. But in the subsequent editions of his textbooks, Simon Simonian felt obliged to note the plagiarization of his textbooks mentioning the name of the plagiarist involved. Armen Anoush had passed away years before Simonian made the notation in the subsequent editions of his history textbooks. His aim was to avert confusing future readers, should they note similarities and identical passages in the contents of the two textbook series.

The ten to twelve lines long notification in his history textbooks remained as a verdict against plagiarism submitted to history and future generations.

5

Simon Simonian's Opus
"Eastern Armenian Literature"

In Simon Simonian's literary legacy there is a piece of work that has always fascinated me with its volume and encyclopedic content. It's an eight hundred-page long book that reminds one of a heavy-set bible. It is titled "Arevelahay Kraganoutiun", "Eastern Armenian Literature", which was published over half a century ago, in 1965 through the sponsorship of Iraqi Armenian writer Levon Shahoyan. It is one of the books I cherish most in my library. I frequently refer to it every time I need information about an Eastern Armenian author.

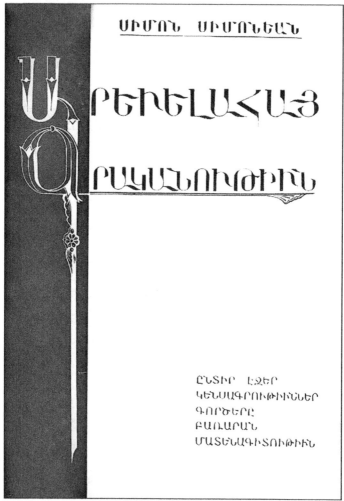

ՍԻՄՈՆ ՍԻՄՈՆԵԱՆ

ԱՐԵՒԵԼԱՀԱՅ

ՕՐԱԿԱՆՈՒԹԻՒՆ

ԸՆՏԻՐ ԷՋԵՐ
ԿԵՆՍԱԳՐՈՒԹԻՒՆՆԵՐ
ԳՈՐԾԵՐԸ
ԲԱՌԱՐԱՆ
ՄԱՏԵՆԱԳԻՏՈՒԹԻՒՆ

"Eastern Armenian Literature"

28

My God, I wonder whenever I refer to the book, how did he manage to gather so much information about Eastern Armenian writers (1850-1920). Within its covers, he assembled information not only about well-known Eastern Armenian writers but also about obscure authors, especially pastoralists whom he unearthed and presented to us.

It is necessary to read the author's fourteen-page long "Introduction" to feel his profound love of our literature in general and of the Eastern Armenian literature in particular.

In his own words, "it is a tribute, a debt of gratitude and love; an attempt to unearth and present Eastern Armenian literature that is one of the five illustrious periods of our millennial old literature". The author believed that Eastern Armenian literature is "much like one of the five arches of the famed Zvartnots Cathedral; outstanding and soaring like an eagle."

According to Simon Simonian, the immortals of Eastern Armenian literature are the following eleven illustrious figures: Novelists Khachadour Apovian, Raffi, Shirvanzade, Mouratsan, Nar-Tos; playwright Gabriel Sountoukian; poets Hovhannes Toumanian, Avedik Isahakian, and Vahan Derian; fairy tales writer Ghazaros Aghayan; and

Avedis Aharonian.

Simon Simonian has presented their extensive biographies with many pictures. He has cited many examples of their most notable and beautiful writings and from other 31 authors, totaling 42. At the end of the massive book, he has listed a dictionary as an addendum, over sixty-two bicolumnar pages, where he has explained the meaning of obscure or unfamiliar words from provincial dialects found in the literary pieces he has presented. The number of words he has listed totals to a staggering 6500 words. In the addendum, he has also listed the chronology of the authors' works. It is a monumental work.

Having studied the Eastern Armenian literature in depth, Simonian has expertly appraised and contrasted it to the Western Armenian literature. Within that context Simonian noted that the Eastern Armenian literature had almost no satirists; it also had not had ecclesiastical writers and almost no female authors, with the exception of Shoushanig Gourghinian. Its counterpart, the Western Armenian literature, boasts of Hagop Baronian and Yervant Odian as satirists; Srvandsyants, Khrimian, Alishan, Archbishop Yeghishe Tourian as authors who were men of cloth; Srpouhie Dusab, Sibil, Zabel Yessayan and Anais as female writers.

Many reviewed and praised Simon Simonian for his exhaustive work about the Eastern Armenian literature. Such reviews appeared in many periodicals such as: "Hask", "Sion", "Pazmaveb", "Hantes Amsoria", "Houssaper", "Spurk" and in other periodicals as well. The reviewers of his book unanimously agreed that his study of the Eastern Armenian literature is much more comprehensive than any other similar study done previously such as Leo's "Russahay Kraganoutiun", "Russian-Armenian Literature", (Venice 1904) or "Russahay Kroghner", "Russian-Armenian Writers", an anthology, (Tibilisi, 1904).

When this impressive volume was being published in the 60's, Simon Simonian used to note in his "Spurk" Weekly that four similar exhaustive works will follow about the four remaining periods of Armenian literature, namely Ancient Armenian Literature from the 5th to the 19th centuries; Western Armenian Literature from 1850 to 1915; Soviet Armenian Literature from 1921 to 1965; and finally Armenian Diaspora Literature from 1915 to 1965.

He passed away in 1986 without these works seeing the light of day.

What had happened? Had he not finished the immense task? Or was it that he found no one to sponsor the publishing of the manuscripts. It is more likely that these intended works had remained in their planning stage.

We have been able to verify only "Badmoutiun Hai Madenakroutian", "History of Armenian Ancient Literature", that was typed as a 70-page long manuscript in 1954 and was henceforth copied and used as a textbook in the seminary of Antelias until the end of the 1960's.

6

The Sassountsi Mountaineers' Twilight in Aleppo

In the mid-1940's, Simon Simonian had barely finished the first three decades of his life living in Aleppo, when he started to pen interesting stories about the daily lives of the Sassountsi mountaineers there. His characters were hard working ordinary folks, who were still entrenched in their ancient ways and customs, spoke in their distinct dialect and had difficulty coping with the demands of their new environment. They compared their everyday living with their ways in their native land. They would not even change attire. They dressed in baggy pants, wore a turban and sandals, grew untrimmed mustaches, and as such would frequently encounter situations in which they felt awkward, if not comical, causing them great discomfort.

Simonian dwelt on these characters. Among them was his own father Ove', who was a miller by trade. He masterfully penned poignant or humorous episodes from their lives. Simon Simonian lived among the characters of the stories he wrote and knew each and every one of them personally. He often engaged in long conversations with them and mined their life stories as the basis for the literature he cultivated then and continued doing so after he moved to Lebanon.

He captivated his readers by his eloquent and moving descriptions of these exiled mountaineers and the longing of their ancient ways. His characters were not fictitious. They were real, in flesh and blood. They lived in Aleppo and Simonian knew them all. He even had them converse in their native dialect in his stories, thus imbuing them with complete authenticity.

"I have never felt the need to resort to the imagination and other literary devices", wrote Simonian referring to his work about the mountaineers of Sassoun "because their lives were inherently more beautiful, authentic, unique and moving than any talented imagination could produce. I have often felt that I do not write these stories, but that the stories write themselves through me as their typewriter".

"The Twilight of the Mountaineers"

Thus his characters with their endearing monikers entered our literature: Porter Uncle Ohan; Tall Artin with his seven daughters; Horseman Ave', who passed away in Aleppo in 1973 at the age of 110; Baker Mano; Aunt Khane'; Lame Sahag; Uncle Magar, the one-time freedom fighter turned into expert bee-keeper; Shoe Mender Levon; Mgro and Deaf Lucine; Bespectacled Magar, and others...

Horseman Ave', who passed away
at the age of 110 in Aleppo in 1973.

The 1915 Genocide had rendered them into exile and had irredeemably stricken them. Away from their ancestral homes, they lived the twilight of their lives.

In 1968 Simonian collected the stories he had written in a book titled "Lernagannerou Verchaluyse", "The Twilight of the Mountaineers". Simonian received many accolades for his book. It was no coincidence that writers in Armenia who hailed from Sassountsi parents were the first to write of their appreciation. In a letter to Simonian, the novelist Khachig Tashdents noted: "The "Twilight", in my opinion, is the dawn of all your literary works in terms of fine art". The poet Vagharshag Norents affirmed that "The Twilight of the Mountaineers" is a true literary work of art. No one has been able to depict the Sassountsi characters in this manner. I admire these characters who remind me of persons dear to me with whom I spent my childhood."

"The Twilight of the Mountaineers" has its own place of honor in my library, especially since it is autographed and personalized by Simon Simonian to one of the characters in the book, shoe mender Levon.

Shoe mender Levon was from Semal village of Sassoun and he was no other than my own paternal grandfather who passed away in 1982.

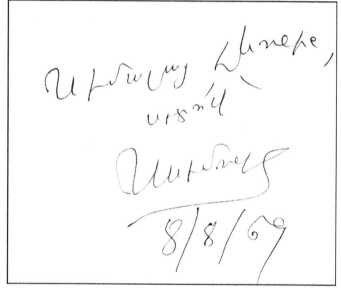

Autograph: "To Levon of Semal, heartily S. Simonian 8-8-69"

7

Simon Simonian's Mother Never Forgot "Her Bédo"

The first story of Simon Simonian's "The Twilight of the Mountaineers" is titled "An Ourish Er", "He Was Different". It is a beautifully articulated moving story. Simonian narrates how his widowed young mother married for the second time but never forgot her deceased husband and kept his memory tenderly and lovingly alive in her heart.

Her first husband's name was Bédo. He was from Dalvoreeg region of Sassoun. He was handsome, daring and generous. He was a miller by occupation. He had come and settled in Aintab where at the age of twenty-five had married Simonian's 17-year old mother to be.

They happily lived together for the next seven years but without being blessed with a child. One day, in 1912, Bédo suddenly fell dead in his mill.

The widowed bride next year married her deceased husband's bosom friend and business partner, Ove' the Miller, who would become Simon Simonian's father.

Simon Simonian narrates that his mother, to the very end of her life (1964) lived with the memory of "her Bédo". She was convinced that the children she conceived in her second marriage were, in fact, Bédo's children "because Bédo always appeared to her the night before conceiving her children and that without Bédo's apparition she never conceived. That is to say, Bédo had become the Holy Spirit…"

Bédo thus, from beyond his tomb, engaged in secret extraterrestrial visits and intrusions disturbing the tranquility of the Simonian household and aggravating Simonian's father Ove'.

One day Simon Simonian asked his mother.

- Bédo did not give you children. You had us from this husband. Do you want Bédo without us or us with our father?

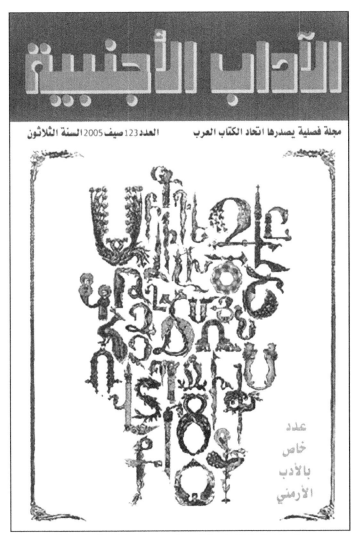

الآداب الأجنبية

مجلة فصلية يصدرها اتحاد الكتّاب العرب   العدد 123 صيف 2005 السنة الثلاثون

عدد
خاص
بالأدب
الأرمني

The Arabic Magazine where Hrach Kalsahakian's
translation of "He Was Different" was published

His mother remained silent for a while then said softly.

- He was different.

Later Simon Simonian wrote a short play in three acts about this topic and included it in his "The Twilight of the Mountaineers" book.

It is fair to note that Hrach Kalsahakian translated this story to Arabic, which was published in the summer of 2005 issue of the Damascus based Arabic magazine "World Literature". That issue was entirely devoted to Armenian literature.

8

Simon Simonian Embraces Teaching

Simon Simonian was born in Aintab (1914) but, as we already noted, part of his roots hailed from Sassoun. His father Ove', who was a miller by trade, was from Germav village of Sassoun.

In his childhood, he witnessed Armenians defending themselves in Aintab. His parents, much like thousands of others, found refuge in Aleppo in 1921 fleeing their persecution in Aintab. In Aleppo, he attended various Armenian schools – "Haigazian", "Giligian Kaghtaganats", "Cilician Refugee's School", and for three years Latin-Catholic schools where the language of instruction was Turkish.

Those were rough years. Aleppo was filled with thousands of Cilician Armenian refugees. Their children, often in rags and barefooted, received an Armenian education and literacy in newly founded modest and impoverished schools.

His father would not tolerate the fact that his son was growing up studying in the Turkish language. Consequently, he took his son out of the Latin school and enrolled him in the newly opened "Grtasirats", "Love of Learning", School where teaching was in Armenian. The year was 1926.

Four years later, in 1930, Simon Simonian graduated from that school. He was already 16 years old.

His quest for learning did not end there.

Right after his graduation, a new opportunity presented itself to Simon Simonian. With a group of adolescent boys from Aleppo, he was accepted to the newly opened Seminary of the Catholicosate of Cilicia in Antelias, Lebanon. He had fifteen classmates. Among them were Zareh Payaslian, the future Catholicos Zareh I; Bishop Terenig Poladian, the future dean of the Seminary; Armen Der Bedrosian, the future principal of Aleppo's Grtasirats School; Nshan Koshafian and Barkev Barsoumian, who became Armenian press correspondents and contributors; Levon Akkhacherian who went by the pen name Zareh

Zarkoun and became a teacher and community activist; Garabed Sabounjian, who became a long standing educator at the Karen Jeppe Jemaran in Aleppo.

Simon Simonian graduated from the Seminary in 1935 having completed its five years long curriculum.

The first graduates of the Seminary of the
Catholicosate of Antelias, Lebanon - 1935

Left to right, sitting: Hovsep Madenian, Stepan Karageozian, Haig Poladian (Arch. Terenig), Garabed Sabounjian, Simon Simonian, Panos Najarian.

Standing, first row: Armen Jerejian, Hagop Bouboushian, Levon Akkhacherian (Zareh Zarkoun), Krikor Bekerejian, Nshan Khoshafian.

Standing, second row: Nshan Sahagian, Yeghishe Varteresian, Armen Der Bedrossian, Barkev Barsoumian, Simon Payaslian (Catholicos Zareh).

He thus attained a deep knowledge of Armenian language, history, and culture. The Seminary had laid down the necessary academic foundation. He showed an inclination and aptitude for academic research. During his years in the Seminary, he accomplished two in-depth studies. One is his vernacular Armenian translation and commentary on the work of the fifth-century historian Movses Gaghangadvatsi "Aghvaneets Badmoutiun", "The History of Aghvan", which he accomplished as a year-end thesis. The manuscript has not been published. The second is about the 19th century Catholicos of all Armenians Kevork IV (1866-1882), which he completed in 1935. The manuscript consisted of 100 pages and was his graduation thesis. The edited manuscript was published in the Catholicosate of Cilicia's monthly "Hask" starting from November 2010 to July-August 2011 in seven consecutive installments titled "Grtoutian Marte Kevork IV-i Metch" – "Kevork IV as an Academician".

***

The Seminary became the last phase of Simon Simonian's education. Henceforth he commenced his teaching career.

After his graduation in 1935, Simon Simonian returned to Aleppo and was appointed as a teacher at the National Haigazian School. His salary was eleven Syrian pounds per month, for eleven months (the 12th-month salary was not paid...). "That is why", he has told Garabed Poladian once, "I know very well that eleven times eleven is 121".

Ardashes Sarkisian (Principle, on the left) and Simon Simonian with the girls' section of the Gulbenkian National School 1939-1941 (?) graduating class in Aleppo, Syria

He taught at the Haigazian School for three years, from 1935 to 1938. Subsequently, he returned and taught for another five years, from 1941 to 1946. In between 1938 and 1941, he taught at the Gulbenkian Armenian School.

Thus, he ended up teaching Armenian language and history for a total of eleven years in Aleppo. During this period he turned down Levon Shant's offer to teach in the Jemaran in Beirut.

Many of the hundreds of students Simonian taught over the years attest that they were profoundly influenced by him, especially in his Armenian history classes when he would speak of the Mamigonian commanders' heroic exploits; the struggles of the Armenian Kings. Simon Simonian's Armenian history textbooks alone make amply evident his reverence of Armenian history. Even today, reading his history textbooks evokes patriotic feelings among young and old.

9

The First Two Issues of "Sevan" Periodical

Among Simon Simonian's legacy in Aleppo, are his printing house "Sevan" and its namesake periodical.

Generally, whenever Simonian's name is mentioned, his "Sevan" publishing house in Beirut automatically comes to mind. He was the founder and sole owner of "Sevan" for decades beginning in 1954.

But if we dig deeper into his biography we will find out that he first founded "Sevan" Printing House in Aleppo in 1945. In this initiative, he had partnered with a few friends and established the "Sevan Publishing Firm". They published literary anthologies such as Levon Pashalian's stories in a volume, a book of selected poems by Vahan Derian and others. But along with these, there were also the two issues of a periodical named "Sevan" that appeared in 1946. The Armenian Teachers' Association of Aleppo had sponsored its publication.

When Simon Simonian published the maiden issue of the "Sevan" periodical, there were two other Armenian literary periodicals in Aleppo. One was Antranig Zarougian's "Nayiri", a monthly that was being published since 1941. The other was "Tebi Yergir", "Towards Homeland", as of 1945, sponsored by a group supportive of Soviet Armenia. Thus, in 1945 there were three Armenian literary periodicals in Aleppo.

I have in my possession the two issues of this "Sevan" periodical. They are 120 & 124 pages long. Prominent Armenian writers of the time have penned articles in these issues. Among them are Catholicos Karekin I Hovsepiants, Nigol Aghpalian, Vahan Tekeyan, Hagop Oshagan, Yeghivart, Aram-Arman, Zareh Melkonian, Smpad Panosssian, Puzant Yeghiayan, Sahag Balekjian, Aris Shaklian, Dr. Haroutiun Der Ghazarian, Vahe-Vahian, Seza, Nerses H. Barsoumian, Yeghia Kassouny and others. Simon Simonian was the editor of these two issues in

The first issue of "Sevan" periodical, Aleppo - 1946

which his stories that would eventually be published in "The Twilight of the Mountaineers" book started appearing. Among these stories, his famed "An Ourish Er", "He Was Different", story appeared in the first issue under a different title.

This periodical devoted to "Literature and Art", unfortunately, had a very short life. Other than these two issues, no others were published because Simon Simonian left Aleppo for Beirut where he would be assigned new responsibilities within the Catholicosate of Cilicia and its Seminary.

10

Catholicos Karekin Invites Simon Simonian to Antelias

The reference in the title is for Catholicos Karekin I Hovsepiants (1943-1952).

He was a distinguished scholar of Armenian studies. He was born in Karabagh in 1867. He was elected Catholicos of the Cilician See in 1943, in wartime. Upon his ascendancy to the throne of the Catholicosate of Cilicia, he made the Catholicosate a cultural center.

One of the first tasks of the newly elected Catholicos was to invite Simon Simonian, the former student of the Seminary, from Aleppo. Simon Simonian was 32 years old then. The Catholicos tasked him with important assignments that Simonian welcomed. Thus Simonian left Aleppo for good and settled in Beirut in 1946.

Simon Simonian was appointed as a tenured lecturer at the Seminary of the Catholicosate in Antelias where he taught classical Armenian and its literature as well as modern Armenian.

The following year, in 1947, the Catholicos appointed him as the Editor-in-Chief of "Hask" Monthly, which is the official organ of the Catholicosate of Cilicia.

He remained at these positions for almost ten years, until 1955.

During those years all the students of the Seminary had the good fortune of being his students. Among them were the future Catholicos Karekin II Sarkissian, Archbishops Ardavast Terterian, Shahe Ajemian, Hrant Khatchadourian and many other priests or lay persons.

Catholicos Karekin II, reminiscing about Simon Simonian's classes, wrote:

"He spoke so ardently about them, (referring to the ancient scribes) that you would think that he was a delegate sent by them as an eloquent lawyer tasked to bring them out of the confines of history to the present, in the current language" ("Spurk" Periodical, Volume 2, 1986).

Along with teaching at the Seminary, Simon Simonian also taught classical Armenian language and ancient Armenian literature at the Hovagimian-Manougian High School for boys and Tarouhi Hagopian High School for girls until 1960. Both of these schools are affiliated with the Armenian General Benevolent Union (A.G.B.U.).

Catholicos Karenkin I Hovsepiants also entrusted him with another important task. The Catholicos assigned him the position of resident-scholar to edit his unpublished scholarly works that were meant to comprise 5 to 6 large volumes. From this sequel, only the first volume was published in 1951.

In the context of the study of ancient manuscripts, in the summer of 1947, Simon Simonian accompanied the Catholicos to Jerusalem where they spent forty days studying the manuscripts kept at the Armenian Patriarchate. Years later, when he reminisced about his time there with the Catholicos, he wrote the following about Karekin Catholicos' love of the ancient Armenian manuscripts; "a young man's first infatuation; a father's love for his son; a grandfather's love of his only grandchild do not adequately reflect Catholicos Karekin's love of the ancient Armenian manuscripts". ("Spurk" Weekly, 6.16.1965).

Furthermore, Catholicos Karekin I entrusted him with

Simonian with His Holiness Karekin Hovsepiants,
Jerusalem - August 1947

another editorial responsibility. The Pontiff had urged the
publication of "Hask Hayakedagan Darekirk", "Hask

Armenological Yearbook". Three consecutive issues were published in 1948, 1951 and in 1957. Bishop Terenig Poladian and Puzant Yeghiayan assisted him in the publication of the first volume; bishop Knel Jerejian assisted him in the publication of the second volume.

Catholicos Karekin Hovsepiants (1st from left) departing from Aleppo after his pontifical visit to Syria in March and April 1946. Three months later, Simon Simonian (1st row, 4th from left), joined the Catholicos in Antelias, Lebanon.

Simon Simonian's tenure at the Catholicosate of Cilicia gave him the opportunity to further his knowledge of

Armenian history and literature. In his interview with Garabed Poladian, Simon Simonian noted the following. "I have read all the ancient authors; the works of all ancient historians with all that has been written about them. I have read cover to cover all issues of "Ararat", the official publication of Etchmiadzin, from 1868 to 1918; also "Pazmaveb" and "Hantes Amsorya" published by the Mekhitarist Order in Venice, and more."

After the death of the elderly Pontiff, a political turmoil swept the Armenian community regarding the Catholicosate of Cilicia that led to polarization, pitting a segment of the community against the other.

In this context, it became difficult for Simon Simonian to carry on his scholarly duties in the Seminary. He was also pondering new ventures, to have his own publishing house and press.

11

"Sevan" Publishing House and 500 Armenian Books

Simon Simonian visited Armenia in the spring of 1954 as a member of the official delegation of the Catholicosate of Cilicia to take part in the internment of Catholicos of All Armenians, Kevork VI Chorekjian. The other members of the delegation were: Archbishop Khat, bishops Terenig, Shahe and Knel, and also poet Vahe-Vahian, Kevork Chatalbashian and Boghos Antoyan.

Armenia was a closed country then. The despotic Stalin had died recently. The proverbial "Iron Curtain" separated Soviet Armenia from the rest of the Armenians in the Diaspora.

Of course, Simon Simonian was setting foot on the Armenian soil for the very first time without realizing that his visit would be the last and that he would never get to visit Armenia again because the authorities would not let him. He returned from Soviet Armenia with mixed feelings that pierced his heart.

Upon his return to Beirut, Simon Simonian founded his own publishing house that in time became not only a commercial enterprise but also an enormous cultural institution. He called it "Sevan" Publishing which, over time, became not only one of the main centers of publication in Lebanon but also a meeting place for the notable writers of the Armenian literary world. Its location on "Ghalghoul Street, No. 36, around the corner from the French Hospital Sacré Coeur" will remain unforgettable in the annals of Armenian book publishing in Lebanon.

In the mid-1950's, when he established "Sevan" Publishing, there were many Armenian printing facilities. The Armenian newspapers ("Aztag", "Zartonk", "Ararat"), the Catholicosate of Cilicia in Antelias, the Hamazkayin Armenian Cultural Association, and the Armenian Catholic press, all had their own printing facilities; not to mention, Atlas, Mshag, Araz, Huys, Donigian, Rotos, Onebar, Edvan and others.

Simon Simonian's "Sevan" Publishing House would be competing against them.

From the very first months, Simonian brought to life his "Sevan" sequel, publishing the voluminous select writings of Yeghishe Charents and Agsel Pagounts (1955).

Soon, grander projects would be launched.

Simon Simonian also ventured into reprinting monumental works such as Prof. Manoug Apeghian's "Hayots Hin Kraganoutian Badmoutiun", "History of Ancient Armenian Literature" (1955-59); Malkhasian's Armenian explanatory dictionary in four volumes (1955-56); Patriarch Ormanian's "Azkabadoum", "Armenian National History", in three volumes (1959-61); Hrachia Ajarian's "Hayots Antsnanounneri Pararan", "Dictionary of Armenian Names", in five volumes (1972) and others. "Sevan" would also print Garo Sassouni's "Badmoutiun Daron Ashkharhi", "History of Daron", (1956); Arshag Alboyajian's "Badmoutiun Malatyo Hayots", "History of the Armenians of Malatia", (1961); Hovhannes Torossian's "Badmoutiun Hai Domarzayi", "History of the Armenians of Domarza", in three volumes (1959-69); Dr. Krikor Astarjian's "Badmoutiun Arapagan Kraganoutian Yev Mshagouyti", "History of Arab Literature and Culture", (1970); Levon L. Luledjian's "Gakavnereh Al Doun Bidi

Chveratarnan", "The Partridges Will No Longer Return Home", (1972); Levon Chormisian's "Hamabadger Arevmdahayots Meg Tarou Badmoutian", "Panorama of a Century of Western Armenian History", the second and the third volumes of the four-volume sequel; and many more such voluminous books.

Not only did Simon Simonian publish the works of eminent and established authors, but also of the young and upcoming ones, such as Vehanoush Tekian, Khosrov Assoyan, Kevork Apelian, Hagop Cholakian, Boghos Kupelian, Levon Vartan, Mikayel Tavrizian, Kevork Temizian and others.

We can safely regard Simon Simonian among the greatest Armenian publishers in Lebanon rivaling the great Armenian publishers of centuries past in Constantinople such as Arabian, Janig Aramian and Muhendisian. During the 27-28 years of its existence, "Sevan" Publishing printed the literary works of 190 authors, in more than 475 titles. An accomplishment that remains unsurpassed.

"Sevan" Publishing continued to print even after the onset of the Lebanese civil war in 1975. It printed some four-dozen books in the next several years. Some of these books were voluminous such as Vazken Antreassian's "Vahan Cheraz Esd Ir Namagneroun", "Vahan Cheraz

According to His Letters", (1977, 544 pages); Hovhannes Shohmelian's translation of William Saroyan's stories; Simon Simonian's "Anjamantros" novel, (1978, 500 pages); Kourken Yazejian's "Abdul Hamid II Garmir Sultane", "Abdul Hamid II, the Red Sultan", (1980, 900 pages); The Sevan Dictionary; Sisag H. Varjabedian's "Hayere Lipanani Metch", "The Armenians in Lebanon", (1981, more than 1100 pages), and others.

Simon Simonian was a prolific writer and his thirst for literature was unquenchable. He professed a deep love of Armenian books. He regarded these books as one of the essential constituents for the preservation of Armenian culture and identity. In 1960 he proposed the following: "Designate the Armenian Martyrs' Day on April 24 as Armenian Book's Day and have the following slogan - to read an Armenian book for every martyr during the Genocide and perpetuate this year after year. If the one million Armenians in the Diaspora would buy and read one Armenian book a year as an offering in memory of a martyr, the legacy of our forefathers would be perpetuated and we would best avenge the victims of the Genocide." ("Spurk" 23.4.1960).

"Sevan" Publishing became another casualty of the Lebanese civil war. It was indiscriminately bombed and sustained massive damages. That part of the capital city became desolate, dangerous and was abandoned. Its last printing became the republication of the Malkhasian dictionary in four volumes in 1983. Next to it was the printing of a large map on the occasion of the 60th anniversary of the Treaty of Lausanne, "as a protest". The map was titled "Badmagan Yev Haverjagan Hayasdan", "Historic and Everlasting Armenia". All the Armenian cities, large and small towns in Eastern and Western Armenia were meticulously mapped. It was the Armenia that Simon Simonian yearned for.

If we were to make a comparison of the Armenian printing in its first three centuries from 1512, when Hagop Meghabard printed the first Armenian book in Venice, to the 1800's, the total number of titled books printed did not exceed one thousand. Simon Simonian single-handedly had around 500 books published.

Experts claim that through its quarter of a century long existence, 16% of all the Armenian books published in Lebanon in that time frame, came from Simon Simonian's "Sevan" Publishing.

Among "Sevan" Publishing's diverse publications, Armenian textbooks had their notable place.

This special concern about Armenian textbooks derived from Simon Simonian's career as a teacher. Surely he was aware of the many challenges teachers face in teaching Armenian history, language, and literature.

We already noted that Simon Simonian taught for eleven years in the Armenian schools of Aleppo. Subsequently, he taught for an additional fourteen years in various Armenian schools in Lebanon.

It is important to note that he was not a mere salaried teacher. He was enthused by teaching and thus embraced teaching for its sake. He regarded teaching Armenian language, literature, and history a mission.

Was there a need for Armenian history textbooks? It was Simon Simonian who filled that important need by preparing and publishing six volumes of Armenian history textbooks starting from Aleppo in 1939 and thereafter in Lebanon.

Were there needs for Armenian language and literature textbooks? It was Simon Simonian again who embarked from 1941 and onward to meet that need. He prepared a sequel of textbooks, laden with pictures, titled "Arakadz" for elementary school children. Onnig Sarkissian (1914-1992), a contemporary and a Sassountsi like him, who also taught Armenian language and literature, collaborated with him and was a co-author in the preparation of these textbooks.

ՕՆՆԻԿ ՍԱՐԳԻՍԵԱՆ ԵՒ ՍԻՄՈՆ ՍԻՄՈՆԵԱՆ

Դ Ա Ս Ա Գ Ի Ր Ք

ՀԱՅԵՐԷՆ ԼԵԶՈՒԻ

Ա. ՏԱՐԻ

Ը. ՏՊԱԳՐՈՒԹԻՒՆ

ՀՐԱՏԱՐԱԿՈՒԹԻՒՆ **ՍԵՒԱՆ** ՀՐԱՏԱՐԱԿՉԱԿԱՆ ՏԱՆ
1 9 7 1 ՏՊ. ՍԵՒԱՆ ՊԷՅՐՈՒԹ

The 8th edition of the Armenian language
textbook "Arakadz" for grade I

Did Armenian schools need Armenian geography textbooks? It was Simon Simonian who heeded the call collaborating with two other educators, Yervant Babayan and Onnig Sarkissian. Beginning in 1956, they produced and published a four-volume geography textbook titled "Ashkharhakroutiun", "Geography".

Moreover, did the schools need Armenian grammar textbooks? It was Simon Simonian who took the initiative, this time partnering with Sarkis Balian to produce and publish in 1967 a two-volume textbook titled "Nor Keraganoutiun", "New Grammar".

Over the passing decades, from 1940's to 1980's, these textbooks were reviewed, were sometimes redesigned and reprinted between eight to ten times. The first two volumes of "Hayots Badmoutiun", "Armenian History", were reprinted in the 1990's and were later reissued with colored pictures by a joint commission of Hamazkayin Armenian Educational and Cultural Society and the Board of Education of the Prelacy of the Armenian Apostolic Church in Lebanon.

Many other authors had their textbooks in religion, science, mathematics, history, drawing, calligraphy, and music printed by "Sevan" Publishing. Simon Simonian thus had great input in this endeavor. He came to be accepted as the authority in the realm of textbooks for Armenian schools. When Western Armenian textbooks prepared in Soviet Armenia became available in Lebanon, it was Simon Simonian who boldly scrutinized their content and pointed their "fatal" and "un-excusable" flaws - (See the ten consecutive issues of "Spurk" Weekly from July 21 to September 29, 1965).

He thus revealed his mind and soul to the Armenian students and Armenian schools.

Educating the adults, including teachers, was no less a concern for him. His voluminous "Arevelahay Kraganoutiun", "Eastern Armenian Literature", book (1965) was, in fact, a scholarly textbook that would be of much help in educating interested adults and teachers alike.

In addition, Simon Simonian embarked on the preparation of another voluminous work. In collaboration with a few intellectuals, he embarked on preparing a modern Armenian dictionary, which he named "Sevan Entartsag Pararan", "Sevan Expanded Dictionary". He toiled for ten years on this project. Its first volume was 740 pages long and was published in 1980 during the Lebanese civil war. It is presumed that a second volume remained incomplete and did not see the light of day.

12

Simon Simonian's "Spurk" Weekly

After founding his own publishing house and after setting it on a sound financial track, the focus of Simon Simonian became having his own newspaper, a dream he had harbored for a long time. He had now attained all that was needed to publish a journal. He had a printing house of his own. He had amassed ample experience in publishing and had a large circle of contributors. He also possessed a vast knowledge, mastered the Armenian language and was a prolific writer.

On April 4, 1958, he published the first issue of his "Spurk", "Diaspora" Weekly.

An issue of "Spurk" Weekly

His initial foray into the publishing of the "Spurk" Weekly appeared to be turbulent. After the first consecutive six issues, the Weekly suddenly ceased being published. 1958 was marred by a fratricidal conflict in Lebanon. Probably that is why he took a break from publishing his Weekly.

In any event, we can consider those six issues experimental, a period of experience in the new endeavor he soon would embark again with full force.

Nonetheless on February 14, 1959, he resumed publishing "Spurk" Weekly numbering it the first issue. He would go on publishing it without interruption for the next eighteen years. The following had articles in this maiden issue – Simon Simonian, Puzant Yeghiayan, Vahram Mavian, Garo Armenian, Kevork Ajemian, Nazaret Patanian, Serop Yeretsian and Krikor Keosseyan.

The Weekly essentially was a literary and a cultural journal. It also reflected on issues that concerned the Armenian Diaspora such as the polarization in the Armenian Apostolic Church between two conflicting camps seated in Etchmiadzin and in Antelias and other ideological and political divides.

"Spurk" Weekly soon had like-minded regular contributors, a large readership in and out of Lebanon. It became a rival of the no less prestigious weekly "Nayiri" that was being published since 1952.

These two journals had identical missions with one being edited by Simon Simonian and the other by Antranig Zarougian. The two ruled as Armenian literary and cultural journals and endeared themselves in the hearts of many. During the times of acute political polarization between the two opposing ideological camps, they became the THIRD VOICE, which was the voice of reason, judicious thinking and for moderation.

On the pages of "Spurk" many reflected on issues that were critically linked with Armenian life and destiny. During the 1960's Simon Simonian penned over twenty editorials demanding the reunification of Karabagh, Na-khichevan and Akhalkalaki to Soviet Armenia. He argued for the foundation of a central Armenian bank in the Diaspora. He saw the need for establishing Armenian Supreme Council to oversee the affairs of the Armenian Diaspora. He urged the non-partisan Armenian masses to emerge from their passivity, narrow political affiliations and be a positive voice of moderation. On an occasion, he noted that, should we be liberating Western Armenia, it would be from the Kurds and not the Turks. His predic-tion proved to be so true given the present day reality on the ground.

Simon Simonian had his own weekly column in the journal. He had many regular contributors: Nshan Khoshafian, Yervant Barsoumian, Yervant Kassouny, Yervant Karajian (Paze'), Levon Vartan, Kevork Ajemian, Haroutiun Garevorian, M.D. (Aghassi), Haroutiun Sa-gherian, M.D., Vazken Etyemezian, Kevork Keshishian, M.D., Armen Donoyan, Arsen Ajemian, Stepan Shahbaz (Alexandria, Egypt), Mikael Gourjian, Khoren Dedeyan, Baruyr Masigian, Haig Jamgochian and Hagop Shahnour (Cairo, Egypt), Koutsi Mikayelian, Vahram Papazian (a former athlete), Puzant Yeghiayan, Hmayag Kranian, Smpad Panossian, Tavit Evereglian, Setrag Zaven (transla-tions from German), Sarkis Ashjian, Krikor Astarjian,

M.D., Zoreeg Mirzayan, Aghasi Hovhannesian, Dev (poet), Onnig Injeyan, Sirvart Injeyan, Garo Poladian, Nshan Beshigtashlian, Yervant Chaprasd, Khosrov Tutunjian, Toros Toranian, Hagop Guloyan, Archbishop Ardag Manougian, Levon Shahoyan, Garo Parseghian, Boghos Kupelian, Aharon Khachadourian, M.D., Aram Shorvoghlian, Dr. Karekin Boujikanian, Anoushavan Frangulian, Hrant Simonian, Dikran Vasilian, Krikor Geovshenian, Kourken Yanikian, cartoonists Diran Ajemian, Hamo Abdalian and from Armenia Hovhannes Shiraz and Sassoun Krikorian and still many others.

"Spurk" Weekly contributors, 1968.
From left to right, Nshan Khoshafian, Yervant Kassouny, Aghasi Hovhannisian, Simon Simonian, Levon Vartan, Smpad Panossian and Yervant Barsoumian

"Spurk" Weekly was not a newsweekly. It was primarily a literary journal. Its 8 to 12 pages would make for an enjoyable reading. Its new year's edition would be special and would be published in 24, 36, 44 or more pages with an incredibly rich content and with many contributing articles. The journal published special issues on other occasions as well, devoting the entire issue to historical events and prominent individuals, such as Saint Mesrob Mashdots, Khorenatsi, Catholicos Zareh I Payaslian, at his death. Along with them "Spurk" Weekly would not miss opportunities to publish special issues about authors such as Kourken Mahari, poet Aharon, Vagharshag Norents, Soghomon Darontsi, Hovhannes Shiraz, Baruyr Sevag (three special issues), Kevork Chavoush, Gomidas, Caloust Gulbenkian, Nerses Shnorhali (at his 800th anniversary), Nshan Beshigtashlian, Yetvart Dasnabedian, April 24 (many special issues), and so on.

Simon Simonian believed that it was necessary to nurture and encourage new and budding writers. For that very purpose, beginning from 1966 and for the next five consecutive years, he periodically published "Spurk-Karoun", "Diaspora-Spring", titled special editions. These issues were devoted exclusively to the literary endeavors of the young and upcoming promising writers. In one of his editorials, Simon Simonian likened the preparations of these issues to the commotion in a beehive. These issues aroused much interest at their times. Some of the "curly" and "newly minted" young writers having started budding on the pages of "Spurk" blossomed, matured and continued to enrich the Armenian Diaspora literature. Some are now established authors in their own rights.

From left to right Simon Simonian and Stepan Shahbaz with some of the young co-editors and writers of "Spurk" Weekly, Kevork Keshishian,M.D., Krikor Keosseyan, Kevork Ajemian and Garo Parseghian in May 1961

Referring to them, Simon Simonian wrote.

"Young writers deserve serious patronage no less than singers and dancers get. There should be a journal for them; there should be opportunities for them to attain higher education, and to travel.

The wealth and the possibilities that our benevolent associations have at their disposal should also be available for the Armenian literature and for those who endeavor in it." ("Spurk" 24.9.1972).

The independent perspective, the unrestrained candor, and sometimes the sharp criticism Simon Simonian expressed in "Spurk" aroused opposition. Opponents to him emerged both in Armenia and in the Diaspora. Often times he confronted his opponents and debated their opposition with sharp commentaries. Sylva Gaboudigian attested to that and noted: "I have a bitter memory of how some of the leaders of the Union of Writers succeeded in coloring the content of "Spurk" Weekly negatively and suddenly our Simon Simonian was converted from a friend to a foe. He was forbidden from entering Soviet Armenia as an undesirable person; so was his Weekly. After that "Spurk" was read in secret" ("Spurk" periodical, May-August, 1999). Fortunately "Spurk" did not falter under pressure and did not alter its orientation. It remained steadfast as an open and daring forum for freedom of thought and speech, always loyal to the aspirations of the Armenians.

It is interesting to note that Simon Simonian had dedicated the leading column of the first issue of "Spurk" to the Armenian government's commendable decision to erect a statue in Yerevan honoring Vartan Mamigonian. He had noted in his column that the statue will come to signify the unbeatable spirit of the Armenians in defense of their Fatherland and would also signify the permanence of their national aspirations.

On December 31, 1974, Simon Simonian wrote his last leading column in "Spurk" Weekly, which he had so ably edited all these past years. He titled his farewell "Fedayeen", "Freedom Fighters". He wrote:

"Patriotism, before anything else, is the liberation of the usurped lands and on those liberated lands establishing the nation. It calls for blood. It also calls for risking all that the people own and galvanizing the consent of all the segments of the population to forge a unity of purpose, a unity of will." Noting that the liberation of Western Armenia could only be possible through the enormous sacrifice of "blood, talents, riches, sweat and ultimately of fedayeen (men of sacrifice)", he asked.

"Where are the progenies of Nemesis and Vahakn?

Where is our Arafat? Where are our Arafats?

Will we be able to change our urban ways and embrace the calling of the fedayeen?"

* * *

In regard to Simon Simonian's "Spurk" Weekly it is important to note that it exuded the freedom loving spirit of the Sassountsis and their love of their mountainous enclave. Simon Simonian was a Sassountsi and he was the longstanding president of the Compatriotic Union of Sassoun.

It is no wonder that his journal became a meeting place for intellectuals whose ancestry hailed from Sassoun or Mush, who crowded the journal with their literary works or their commentaries. Some of them were: Vagharshag Norets, Khachig Tashdents, Soghomon Darontsi, Sassoun Krikorian, Roza Bedrosian, Vartan Bedoyan, Hmayag Kranian, Karekin Yeretsian, M.D., Levon Carmen, Kevork Ajemian, Ardashes Donjoyents, Mikael Tavrizian and others.

* * *

The average number of the subscribers to "Spurk" Weekly was 1500. One-third of them were in Lebanon and the rest in Syria and abroad. The Weekly was banned in Armenia.

Simon Simonian edited "Spurk" Weekly for 16 years, until the end of December 1974. Henceforth, he wanted to devote his time to his various literary and scholarly projects. He passed on the responsibility to his brother-in-law Kevork Ajemian (1932-1998).

The days were becoming gloomy.

Within months the civil war in Lebanon erupted, which would last for the next fifteen years. Ajemian would be able to publish "Spurk" for two years, in 1975 and in 1978 with unavoidable interruptions.

During 1985, 1986 and 1988, three issues of "Spurk" were published as periodicals. Kevork Ajemian, at the end of 1989, transferred "Spurk" to the Armenian Popular Movement. The latter published it as a monthly with an altogether different format and content.

The entire collection of "Spurk" Weekly with a complete bibliography was prepared and published by Lebanese Armenian intellectual Sako Oknayan, in 1984, in Beirut. It is refreshing to find out that, lately, the issues of "Spurk" were digitized in Armenia and can be accessed online.

Every now and then I feel the urge to peruse the fading issues of "Spurk" Weekly. There are so many articles there that make for enjoyable reading even today. "Spurk" Weekly is the affirmation of the Armenian Diaspora during the 1960's and 1970's. It is a reflection of the era by the best and brightest.

I can guarantee you that on the yellowed pages of "Spurk" Weekly a person would find more captivating subjects than in the current journals; especially because these articles were penned with an impeccable Western Armenian that is already getting irreversibly relegated to history.

13

Simon Simonian's First Novel

Simon Simonian's first novel is titled "Geh Khntrvi Khachatsevel", which literally means, "Please Overlap", that is to say, organize another event on the same date, at the same time and within the same community to cross with the one already planned. It was his first novel, which was published in 1965.

We already know that his voluminous scholarly work, "Arevelahay Kraganoutiun", "Eastern Armenian Literature", was also published in the same year.

Simonian was already 51 years old when he published his first novel. Therefore we can perhaps note that he was

ՍԻՄՈՆ ՍԻՄՈՆԵԱՆ

ԿԸ ԽՆԴՐՈՒԻ... ԽԱՉԱՁԵՒԵԼ

ՀԱՅ ԺՈՂՈՎՈՒՐԴԻ ԾՆՆԴԵԱՆ

10000-ԱՄԵԱԿԻ ՏՕՆԱԿԱՏԱՐՈՒԹԻՒՆԸ

● ԱՌԱՋԻՆ ՕՐ ●

Հ Ա Յ Ո Ց

Ե Ր Դ Ի Ծ Ա Կ Ա Ն

Պ Ա Տ Մ Ո Ւ Թ Ի Ւ Ն

ՏՊ. ՍԵՒԱՆ

1965

ՊԷՅՐՈՒԹ

"Please Overlap"

late in introducing it to the public. The reason most likely was that he was busy editing the literary works of others. For years he had spent time and effort editing Catholicos Karekin I's manuscripts, the periodicals "Hask" and "Spurk", the voluminous projects of his "Sevan" Publishing firm. Even publishing his "Lernagannerou Verchaluyse" book, whose stories he had written during 1945-47, was delayed for a couple of decades and was not published until 1968.

"Geh Khntrvi Khachatsevel", was conceived by a very interesting idea or a vision. It relates a fictional event that can arouse the interest of those who are familiar with Armenian history and know the distinct personalities of its luminaries and heroes.

What is the subject?

Simon Simonian invites us to attend a gala celebrating the TEN MILLENNIA OF THE ARMENIAN PEOPLE that is taking place in the UNESCO hall, the biggest in Lebanon. An "All Armenians United Organization" has organized the event. In the hall, sitting next to each other are the who's who of Armenian history. They are present in a special, beyond the grave, get together.

The gala will last three days and will have more or less the following program.

Krikor Lousavorich, Catholicos Sahag Bartev, King Ashod I Pakradouni will alternately preside over the program.

The following will come onto stage and will deliver their speech on their subjects that will include: The patriarch of the nation Haig on, "Why did I flee to the country of Ararat"; Dikran the Great on, "Why did I venture outside the borders of Armenia"; King Drtad on, "Why did I change religion for the sake of a woman"; Vasak Siuni on, "Why did I side with the Persians".

The following will recite: Mesrob Mashdots, "Ayp, Pen, Kimeh", "The A, B, C"; Sahak Bartev, "Ororeh", "The Lullaby"; Ghevont Yerets, "Ankgh Kughin Yerkeh", "The Ankgh Village Song"; Father Kirakos, "Aniyee Panalinereh", "The Keys of Ani". Father Gomidas Vartabed will give the concluding remarks.

In attendance, there will be great international guests such as Pel of Babylon, Lucullus, Pompeius, Caesar Augustus, Nero, Hazgerd II, Nestor, Alpaslan, Genghis Khan, Timour Lenk, Shah Abbas, Queen Tamara, Gladstone, Sultan Hamid, Talaat, Enver, Stalin and Beria, all linked to Armenian history.

They will address the following topics:

- What did we do to the Armenian people?

- Why did not the Armenian people perish?

- Why will the Armenian people not die?

The traditional Armenian political parties will see that the event is run in a secure and orderly manner. The bells will be entrusted to the Hnchag Party; the guns to the Tashnag Party; and the silence to the Ramgavar Party. There will be fund raising to support the A.G.B.U. In the morning there will be requiem service to the souls of future martyrs, presided by the pagan priests of Ashdishad and Yeriza.

It is asked that you note the date and the time of this gala and cross it by another function.

* * *

Would you not have liked to be present and hear what these historical characters have to say?

Simonian's partly comedic, partly philosophical and allegorical, but primarily a histographic book engages the reader.

In fact, it is theatrical, (or semi-theatrical) wherein some of the greats of the Armenian history come onto stage in front of the audience and defend, explain or bare their actions.

For example, let us hear this excerpt from what Queen Shamiram of Assyria confided after greeting the audience.

"Ara refused my love. I had promised him my kingdom along with my heart. He would have become the king of two countries, the kingdom of Ararat and Assyria because these two countries would have ceased fighting each other to extinction. Handsome Ara rejected both the throne and my heart.

Had Ara joined me, the great majority of the oil wells of Mosul, some 95%, would have belonged to the Armenians. With Calouste Gulbenkian's 5%, the Armenians would have owned all. Just for the sake of Nvart Khanum, Lady Nvart, Ara lost two kingdoms and the oil wells of Mosul".

Similarly, a really interesting scene is revealed to us when governor Vasak Siuni ascends to the stage and demands to cross-examine on stage the 5th century historians Goruyn Skancheli, Magnificent Goruyn, Yeghishe, Ghazar Parbetsi, as well as our contemporaries Professor Nikolai Adonts and Hrant K. Armen. He then obliges them to read excerpts from their historical textbooks having to do with him – Vasak Siuni.

It is revealed that Goruyn's and Parbetsi's accounts are positive about Vasak and it is only Yeghishe's account, which is negative about him all along, for rather opaque reasons.

In another instance, the author creates an intimate conversation between Pel of Babylon and Stalin. The latter says: "You know Comrade Pel, I invented worship of the individual. I made them worship me. To be worshipped, it is necessary to create fear. The history of religions shows us that many of the gods were worshipped because of fear. So you and I imposed fear and worship."

The book fails in some segments; in some points, it lags and stagnates despite the author's wit and strong imagination.

Simon Simonian had planned to make this a sequel of three volumes. The other two volumes were written but were not published separately. Much later, Simon Simonian planned to re-edit and publish all three volumes but this extensive work remained incomplete.

It is obvious that Simon Simonian's inspiration for this work is his knowledge of Armenian history as evidenced by his history textbooks. This book is the echo of these textbooks wherein, Simon Simonian at times with some satire and with some tears ponders why, what happened and how is it that the Armenians endured but remained a small nation?

It would have been worthwhile for our playwrights to consider staging this book.

By the way, the great Soviet Armenian actor and director Vartan Ajemian (1905-1977), during a visit to Lebanon in 1966 as the head of the Sundukyan Theater, referring to Simon Simonian's work had noted "It's a masterpiece. Had he gone along with our leadership, I could have staged this in Moscow and showed to our 15 republics that we also have theater."

14

The Fate of the Mountaineers

In the 1960's Simon Simonian periodically also wrote in prose many other literary meritorious pieces that were assembled in two volumes in 1967 and 1970 titled, "Sipana Kacher", "Daredevils of Sipan". Earlier he had written many other moving stories about the Sassountsis.

These stories were taken from aspects of Diaspora life.

In 1972 Simon Simonian published a collection of select pieces from his writings in a voluminous book he titled "Ler Yev Jagadakir", "Mountain and Destiny". The volume comprised of all the stories in his "Lernagannerou Verchaluyse" book and select pieces from his two volumes of "Sipana Kacher". In total, a 475-page long magnificent

"Mountain and Destiny"

book was produced that any author could be honored for.

Years ago when I was a student at the Karen Jeppe Jemaran I borrowed this book from the school's library and read it partly.

Naturally, after many decades I do not remember all the stories I read. For that reason, a desire to reread the book gnawed my soul.

I borrowed a copy of the book from the community center's library, immersed myself in its pages and read it "calmly and gently" as our eminent poet Vahan Tekeyan would say.

It is a book that can be read with one breath. In my opinion "Ler Yev Jagadakir" is a timeless literary work. Reading it would be an enlightening experience for any reader for many reasons.

First and foremost, the language is in impeccable Western Armenian. It is ornate and uplifts a reader. Alas, one cannot find such an eloquent spoken and written language anymore.

I became convinced that the stories of the "Sipana Kacher" are no less appealing and masterfully written than the stories in the "Lernagannerou Verchaluyse" book. Each and every one of them is distinct and impressive.

"Mayrig, Mayrig", "Mamma, Mamma", depicts a

mother, a Genocide survivor, who travels from Aleppo to the U.S.A., to visit her only son and faces neglect and contempt by her daughter-in-law, grandchildren, and assimilated relatives.

"Hai Meh", "An Armenian", is the story of two Armenians who serendipitously meet each other on a street in Copenhagen and right away are connected. Hans Nalbandian, a high placed Danish government official, laments the fact he cannot read Armenian. The episode is real. The protagonist is the son of onetime principal of the Getronagan Varjaran of Constantinople, Mardiros Nalbandian from Sepastia and his Danish wife Inga.

"20,000-en Megeh", "One of the Twenty Thousand", is the story of an Armenian officer in the German army who frees a Soviet Armenian prisoner of war from certain doom. Twenty years later the freed prisoner, now the president of a prestigious scientific company in the United States, comes to Berlin to look for his savior to thank him for having saved his life.

Read "Tourk Kntabedi Meh Hed", "With a Turkish Colonel"; "Atatourken Aghchegeh", "Ataturk's Daughter", to pierce through the deepest and most secret folds of a Turkish man's psychology.

Furthermore, read "Gagh Zinvorin Badmoutiuneh",

Simon Simonian in front of "Sevan" publishing & printing house,
the year he published his "Mountain and Destiny" book in 1972.

"The Story of the Lame Soldier", an amazing story and you will utter "unbelievable but true".

Much like his previous works, "Ler Yev Jagadakir" was also well received by the intellectual elite and the general reading public. The only dissenting voice came from the Armenian novelist Arek Dirazan (1902-1987), who had formerly resided in Istanbul. He wrote a lengthy criticism of the book in consecutive issues of "Zartonk" Daily, pointing out the author's "linguistic errors".

Simon Simonian did not sit idle. In six consecutive issues of "Spurk" (October 7 to November 10, 1974), he denied the allegations with irrefutable proof, while simultaneously delivering a lesson in Armenian language and vocabulary.

15

Pursuing Big Projects

Simon Simonian always pursued big pan-Armenian projects believing in their necessity and especially in the possibility of their realization. However, these projects were so big that a single person's lifetime would not have been enough for their realization.

Two or three years before his death, during the raging civil war in Lebanon, he got engaged in a series of dialogues with the French Armenian writer Garo Poladian who was staying in Lebanon at the time. Simon Simonian revealed to him his vision for the future of Armenia and the Armenian people. Their exchanges had lasted for months as Simonian explained and formulated his ideas and Poladian took notes. Fate interrupted this dialogue as both writers unexpectedly passed away in the same year, in 1986, Simonian in March and Poladian in May.

Nonetheless, Armen Tarian took stewardship of Garo Poladian's notes and had them published in 1988, which became the 6th and last volume of Garo Poladian's series titled "Zruyts", "Dialogue".

From left to right Armen Tarian, Yervant Kassouny and Simon Simonian - December 1984

This long narrative sheds light not only on Simon Simonian's life and his literary legacy but also puts on the agenda of the critical issues that shook the Armenian

Կ. ՓՈԼԱՏԵԱՆ

ՕՐՈՅՃ

Զ. ՀԱՏՈՐ

ՍԻՄՈՆ ՍԻՄՈՆԵԱՆԻ ՀԵՏ

ՊԷՅՐՈՒԹ 1988

Garo Poladian's "Zruyts" sequel, Volume VI, with Simon Simonian

nation during the previous six decades. It examines the issue of the nation's survival and perpetuation. As such Simonian critiques, submits proposals, and formulates solutions to the issues. He was a deeply concerned patriot, always original and independent as an intellectual. At one point he notes:

"The Armenian people with boundless patience and trust, for almost a century let the political parties try to achieve their mission. But they didn't succeed. During their endeavors, we lost Western Armenia. For the first time in 4000 years, there are no Armenians left in Western Armenia. This fact is horrible. Since 1915, there are no Armenians in the largest parts of Armenia. There are no Armenians in Alashgerd, Gars, Garin, Erzenga, Khnous, Daron-Dourouperan, Vasbouragan, Kharpert, and furthermore in Dikranagerd and in the whole of Western Armenia. One needs to be a historian to deeply appreciate this indescribable and immeasurable truth and one needs to muster one's heart to accept the ones who lost these as saviors" ("Zruyts" Volume VI, page 107-108).

The Sassountsi daredevil, ended his narrative saying "I wish 100 years from now, in 2085, we would be given the opportunity to resurrect from our graves for a moment and open our eyes to see if Armenians still exist; and how do they live? I believe that in 2085 the 15 provinces of historic Armenia will be full of Armenians and the grandchild of my grandchild will be in Germav, my father's hometown village in Sassoun and is a worker in a factory there".

Seizing the moment at the occasion of the 70th commemoration of the Genocide, Simonian had found it to be an opportune time to publish the essence of his views he had articulated in his dialogue with Garo Poladian. In a series of articles in "Zartonk" Daily, spanning from April 10 to May 23, 1985, he had them published titled, "Our Sublime Tasks for the Eternity of the Armenian People". The series was a message to readers to heed his call.

Did he have listeners? Was he heard?

Simon Simonian's literary and publishing projects were many and grand. After the shutting down of "Sevan" Publishing, we see Simon Simonian in 1984 as one of the four partners for a new publishing venture. In spite of his advancing age and fatigue, the publishing spark had remained in him. It is said that ink also circulated with his blood.

Those close to him relate that in his last years, because of his advancing age, or because of the havoc brought upon him by the civil war in Lebanon, Simon Simonian had the psychology and pace of a man in a hurry. Something had shattered in him; especially that "Sevan" Publishing had to close its doors against his will. His health often betrayed him. He seemed to have become more irritable with the passing of time. His projects had outpaced him and he was not able to catch up with them.

Simonian as seen by the famous
Egyptian Armenian caricaturist Alexander Saroukhan - 1962

"There is a lot to be done. We are running late, real late", he would often say.

Indeed he had remained late to conclude some projects he had nurtured.

He had wanted to re-edit "Geh Khntrvi Khachatsevel" book and expand it to three volumes. He had already written 150 additional pages. However, the project did not come to fruition.

He had planned to add to his "Arevalahay Kraganoutiun", a book he had published in 1965, four volumes of supplements in a sequel, adding the following periods: Classical (ancient), Western Armenian Literature, Soviet Armenian Literature and Diaspora Literature. Not even the Western Armenian Literature supplement, which he had announced in the press "was ready" saw the light of day.

The second volume of the "Sevan Entartsag Pararan", "Sevan Expanded Dictionary", (1980) did not see the light of day either, even though he had the assistance of Garo Sarafian and Manuel Keoseyan.

According to him, he had completed the manuscript of a book that would have been twenty-four chapters, titled "Kerezman Chdarvelik Paner", "Things Not to Be Taken to the Grave", relating to memories from his childhood. It would have been two hundred pages long. This too, did not see the light of day. Chapters from this book were published in 1983 in "Nor Hai" a journal in Los Angeles and in the 1984-85 issues of "Nor Ayntab" periodical in Beirut.

He had in mind to write in his memoirs about celebrated personalities such as Catholicos Karekin Hovsepiants, Hagop Oshagan, Arshag Alboyajian, Arshag Chobanian, Nigol Aghpalian, Gostan Zarian and others. He was not able to do it.

He had wanted very much to have a collection of one hundred of his selected editorials in "Spurk", an anthology of sorts, published as a book. This did not happen either.

As early as in 1930's, Simon Simonian had focused his attention on Vartan Aykegtsi, an Armenian author of fables who lived in the 12th century. Simon Simonian published a scholarly work about him in Arshag Chobanian's "Anahid" periodical. After further research, Simon Simonian had concluded that some of the fables of Jean De La Fontaine, 17th century, were taken directly from Vartan Aykegtsi's book of fables, "Aghvesakirk", "Fox's Book". Simon Simonian expanded on the subject and wrote an essay titled "Vartan Aykegtsi and La Fontaine". The manuscript has not been published.

Another scholarly paper made a comparison of the writ-

ings of Khorenatsi in the fifth century and Anania Shira-
gatsi in the seventh century. Simon Simonian, citing many
examples, had noted many similarities in their literary
legacies, an interesting and useful scholarly work that has
remained incomplete.

In his later years, he had decided to list ten distinct
topics of Armenian history and culture (such as science,
architecture, painting, military personalities, important
cities, beautiful landscapes of Armenia, etc.) and present 10
GREATS or 10 WONDERS in each category. He had
prepared the list of names, but the work did not
materialize.

He planned to write a thousand pages long history of
Armenian literature in Syria and in Lebanon during the
past sixty years, presenting its evolution, notables, and
accomplishments. He had found loyal collaborators, (Armen Tarian, Jirayr Tanielian, Yervant Barsoumian), although he was to shoulder most of the task. Thus, the
project had a body and structure and he even had posted
an appeal in the media to that effect (August 1980), but
the project was not accomplished and remained incomplete.

He dreamed of publishing the Western Armenian literature in ONE HUNDRED volumes, much like the
British Nelson Publishing, presenting the biographies of

the authors, their literary genres, accompanying each with a glossary. He had laid down the groundwork for the project and had even applied to individuals to be the Maecenas of the project. It did not happen.

As did much, much more…

16

Simon Simonian's Posthumous Novel

Among his varied literary interests, Simon Simonian also wrote novels.

Almost a year before his death he had started writing a novel based on the life experiences of the members of his family and close friends. He wrote some 50 to 60 pages then paused.

This was not his first foray into novel writing.

He already had written a 500-page long novel titled "Anjamantros" and had it printed in his own facility in 1978. It is an odd title, with a strange content and also had a whimsical fate.

Although the novel was printed in his lifetime, it was

his wish that the novel is distributed only after HIS DEATH.

No one knows why he had made such a provision.

"Anjamantros" - The person who is living beyond his times.

Consequently, hundreds of copies of the printed books were stored in boxes, remaining dormant in the "Sevan" Publishing storage for the next eight years, until his death in March 1986. Until then he had allowed only a handful of close intellectual friends to read the "mysterious" novel on condition that they would not express their opinions to the public. Among the few was Garo Poladian, who reviewed it in the sixth volume of "Zruyts" having found the book captivating and praiseworthy.

Thirty years after Simonian's death, as I write these sentences, let it be known that I recently procured a copy from our Kristapor Library and read the book patiently from the very beginning right to the very end.

 Should you ask me, why did Simonian keep it under lock during his lifetime, his most extensive literary work? I will be hard pressed to formulate a convincing and a logical justification.

What were the reasons that the author forbade his printed novel from seeing the light of day in his lifetime? Why did he choose to erect an artificial wall between him and the multitude of readers who cherished reading his works? How did he endure his stubbornness in keeping a cooked dish in the refrigerator for so long, so to speak?

It was a wrong and an unjustifiable act. It was a steadfast Sassountsi dare devilish act.

Because, when the locks of the boxes were removed after his death, the novel did not generate the expected interest. On the contrary, it met an indifferent public. Almost nothing has been written about the novel in the Armenian press at the time. Alas.

I am inclined to think that the fate of "Anjamantros" would have been far better had it been published when he was alive. Interpretations, analysis critiquing would have followed one after another. Perhaps there would have been public causeries. The author would have been there to give his views and offer his explanations. Nothing of that sort happened.

What does "Anjamantros" mean? According to the author, this original word is a compound word. "Anjam" in Armenian means not timely. "Antros" means a person in Greek. Therefore "Anjamantros" means a person who is living beyond his times.

The novel has an unusual structure. The protagonist of the novel is an architect named Arsen Zamanian who experiences a whirlwind of interesting developments while at the same time he is engaged in writing his own novel, the content of which, in all its details, is linked to the unfolding of the main novel thus making a BIFURCATED NOVEL. It is a novel within a novel.

Therefore, within the covers of the book, the reader finds two novels, one is real while the other is unreal. The main protagonist of the unreal novel is Anjamantros who embodies more than one person and is reincarnated having lived 9999 years earlier. He is the archetypal Man with his vanities and virtues. He might be the archetypical Armenian with his weaknesses, successes, vacillation, and ability to reincarnate. In the pages of the novel, we encounter a hypocrite, a girl who prostitutes herself for the sake of livelihood, a usurer, an ingrate, a wrestler who knocks down oak trees but is impotent with his wife, brothers who devour each other for the sake of money, etc.

Allegorical scenes are abundant in the novel because Simon Simonian has at times the unreal and the real protagonists face each other. It is difficult to fully understand the perspectives of the author. There are repetitions and redundancies that weigh down the flow of the narration loosening the engagement of the reader. But in most of its parts, the novel flows smoothly, including a romantic theme that threads from the beginning to its shocking tragic end.

There is an overt disdain of communism in the novel. The main heroine, Alia Gasian, is an Iranian national and a devout communist. On one occasion she rants in despair.

"Communism, which we thought is the last prescription to end humanity's misery, is far from making mankind happy. It has not even succeeded in curing the basic ailments of prehistoric man, such as fear and need. Instead of lavishing real joy to the people, it has deluded them into accepting the illusion of being happy, which is far from rendering people to be joyful. Communism has not even been able to teach LOVE. It has eliminated love from the hearts". (See page 455).

Another hero named Kolia, Alia's fiancé, is also a committed communist and a revolutionary agent, who confesses in his turn.

"Communism could not make people happy. Whoever thinks differently, is a liar. A person receiving a salary of 100 rubles but spending 300 rubles cannot afford not to lie, not to deceive and not to steal. This reality by itself refutes every myth." (See page 473).

"Anjamantros" was published in Armenia as well in 1998. Its publication was sponsored by writer Apkar Apinian and was supported by the Writers Union of Armenia. It was published in standard Western Armenian diction.

Unfortunately, this publication also met the same fate as the novel's maiden print in Lebanon. There was hardly any reflection of it in the literary press.

17

Simon Simonian Hosted in the United States of America

It was 1983.

Simon Simonian was on the cusp of his 7th decade. It was high time that his literary, educational, editorial and publishing legacy be recognized publically. To be fair, it was due to him.

Such an initiative, above all, was expected from the Lebanese Armenian community wherein he had toiled for over 35 years. Or else, given the prevailing conditions of civil war in Lebanon, the Aleppo Armenian community, which was enjoying stability and peace, could have taken the initiative. Aleppo was Simon Simonian's genuine "home". It was there that he had received his elementary education and had taught there for ten years. The heroes of his stories were the Sassountsis who had lived in Aleppo. At the very least it could have been the Daron-Dourouperan Compatriotic Union in Aleppo actualizing such homage to his career. It is the only organization that Simon Simonian had ever joined. But, there was no thoughtful person left.

Soviet Armenia continued to ignore him. Yerevan did not look favorably to this Sassounti daredevil.

It was Armenian Americans who took the initiative and put things in motion. His former grateful students and the former contributors of "Spurk" came together and organized a committee to plan celebrations in three cities with the assistance of The Armenian Literary Group of Los Angeles under the Chairmanship of Hrant Simonian.

Simon Simonian thus departed to the United States.

Armen Tarian, one of his close friends, noted.

"It was with much joy that he embarked on his journey to America although a few months earlier he had suffered a heart attack. It was a miracle that he had pulled through. The doctors had advised him to stay away from things that would fatigue him or cause him emotional upheavals.

Wherever he went he inspired much enthusiasm and belief in "the eternity of the Armenian people, at the cost of straining himself" ("Shirag" Monthly 1989, No. 8-9).

Across the United States, there were approximately twenty meetings with him but the main events were three.

Simonian on his arrival day to Los Angeles, March 11, 1986.
From left to right, Yervant Kochounian,
Simon Simonian and Hrant Simonian.

The first one took place in Los Angeles on March 13, 1983. The master of ceremony was Oshin Keshishian. Yervant Kochounian, Vehanoush Tekian, Haroutiun Sagherian, M.D. and Zareh Zarkoun took to the podium and presented Simon Simonian's legacy.

A 60-page long booklet was prepared for the occasion with appropriate content.

The flyer inviting the public to attend Simon Simonian's celebratory tribute in Los Angeles, Ca.

The second public event took place in New York City on April 9. The main speakers were Fr. Karnig Halajian, Fr. Antranig Kasparian, (Simon Simonian's former students in the Seminary), Noubar Kupelian and Antranig Poladian.

The jubilee celebration in Philadelphia took place on April 15th. The Tekeyan Cultural Association hosted the event. The two speakers were Koutsi Mikayelian and Antranig Poladian.

At all the venues, there were artistic performances and presentations of his literary legacy. The American Armenian press devoted ample space reporting on Simon Simonian's visit.

Simon Simonian had never aspired for glory. He was a modest representative of his generation. He returned from America to Beirut recuperated spiritually and enthused with new plans. However, Armen Tarian noted that Simon Simonian was disappointed by the indifference of the Lebanese Armenian press. Armen Tarian would then go on repeating the old adage:

"The only place where the prophet is not honored is in his hometown".

ԹԷՔԷԵԱՆ ՄՇԱԿՈՒԹԱՅԻՆ ՄԻՈՒԹԻՒՆ
ƮEKEYAN CULTURAL ASSOCIATION
ՖԻԼԱՏԵԼՖԻՈՅ ՄԱՍՆԱՃԻՒՂ   **OF PHILADELPHIA**

*Tekeyan Cultural Association of Philadelphia
cordially invites you to attend*

ՅՈԲԵԼԵԱՐ
ՍԻՄՈՆ ՍԻՄՈՆԵԱՆ

A Tribute to
Simon Simonian

*Noted Educator, Scholar, Author and Editor
on a brief visit to the United States*

Friday, April 15, 1983 — 8:30 P.M.
St. Sahag — St. Mesrob Cultural Hall

ՄԵԾԱՐԱՆՔ

ՍԻՄՈՆ ՍԻՄՈՆԵԱՆԻ

(Ուսուցիչ, բանաստէր, գրող եւ խմբագիր)
Միացեալ Նահանգներ այցելութեան առիթ

Նախագահութեամբ`
ԶԱՒԷՆ Ծ. ՎՐԴ. ԱՐՁՈՒՄԱՆԵԱՆԻ

Master of Ceremonies
Arpi Simonian

Greetings by
Koudsy Mikaelian   and   Antranig Poladian

Program Presided by
Very Rev. Zaven Arzoumanian

Եթէ կրնաս` բարձրացի՛ր, բայց զիսել՛ս ո՛ւր, մինչեւ ա՛ւր,
եւ Ճեզի ճետ ուրիեն՛ն` եթէ կրնաս` բարձրացո՛ւր..... ՎԱՀԱՆ ԹԷՔԷԵԱՆ

18

Simon Simonian's Will and Death

Three years after the accolades he received in the United States by a grateful community, Simon Simonian bid his farewell to this world on March 24, 1986.

In his last years, the specter of death had pursued him. "I have started dreading that day; its actuality, its imminence, its suddenness, and its finality", he wrote with an anxious pen in "Gantch" Biweekly on February 20, 1983.

He left behind a strange and an out of the ordinary will.

It was strictly a "personal" will. Simon Simonian married Marie Ajemian in 1946. The couple was blessed with five children – Hovig, Maral, Vartan, Daron and Sassoun. He had stipulated that other than his immediate family members, no one else is present at his interment.

And so it was.

His funeral service was performed in the Saint Krikor Lousavorich Cathedral in the courtyard of the Catholicosate of Cilicia in Antelias. It presented the last chance for those who wanted to pay homage to the memory of this last mountaineer. Among them foremost stood, the Catholicos Karekin I Sarkissian, the former student of the deceased.

In the Cathedral the Pontiff gave an eloquent eulogy emphasizing "One of the greatest virtues of Simonian, as I have known him, was his ability to invite others to the fields where he was laying furrows. Now I imagine how many tens of students with his encouragement, embraced the Armenian letters and through the Armenian media and by personal publications enriched the culture".

Forty years of productive life in the Lebanese Armenian community thus came to its end (1946-86).

Simon Simonian's legacy in its entirety is extraordinarily big and heavy.

He was hard working with diverse pursuits. Satirist Dikran Vassilian had likened "Sevan" Publishing, Simon Simonian's "purgatory" where he toiled 25 hours a day with "his feet in his shoes" and with an Alishanian diligence and an abbot's endurance. It was customary for him to work on 4 to 5 projects at a time.

Referring to Simon Simonian's legendary hard working habit, the Egyptian Armenian satirist Baruyr Masigian mentions the following:

"On an occasion, I asked him. When did you manage to accomplish these enormous tasks?

Simon Simonian answered with a smile:

- The late poet Vahan Tekeyan has made a special notation to me.

- What?

- "From midnight to early morning"".

* * *

Perhaps Simon Simonian did not receive the recognition he deserved for his literary accomplishments. Sometimes he was deliberately ignored.

For example, literary critic Minas Tölölyan ignored Simon Simonian in his revised 1977 edition of "Tar Meh Kraganoutiun", "A Century of Literature". He had made room for the former students of Simon Simonian – Kevork Ajemian, Vehanoush Tekian, Boghos Kupelian – but had kept a stony silence when it came to Simon Simonian.

The attitude of the Soviet Armenian Encyclopedia is no less scandalous. Its editors elected to leave Simonian out from its twelve-volume sequel.

On the other hand in the United States, Seta Demirjian in her "Spurkahay Arti Kraganoutiun", "Contemporary Armenian Diaspora Literature", (1994, second edition), gave due recognition to Simon Simonian's literary legacy.

After independence, "Ov e Ov", "Who's Who", a biographical directory printed in Armenia included Simon Simonian in its 2007 edition (second volume).

Admittedly there has been much interest in Simon Simonian after his death. Remembrances were organized in Aleppo, which I mentioned at the beginning; in Beirut, at the first anniversary of his death in 1987 and another in 2014; in Yerevan in 1999 at his 85th birthday celebration. "Spurk" periodical (New Period) devoted its second issue (1986) to Simon Simonian; so did "Shirag" Monthly in 1989.

Two monographs have been published about him. One by Sassoun Krikorian in Yerevan and is titled "Pazmadaghant Yerakhdavoreh", "The Multi Talented Benefactor", (1999, 104 pages); the other by Toros Toranian in Aleppo and is titled "Simon Simonian Yerevouyteh", "Simon Simonian, The Phenomenon", (2004, 240 pages). An-

"Shirag" Monthly - Issue # 8-9, 1989

tranig Dakessian penned a scholarly study on the Armenian textbooks published by Simon Simonian's "Sevan" Publishing. The study was presented in a book published by Haigazian University in 2014. Assadour Guzelian in London published in 2014 a collection of his correspondence with his former teacher Simon Simonian, totaling some fifty letters. Hagop Cholakian in his sixth volume of "Antasdan" textbook (2014) series about the Armenian language and culture, presented a story from Simon Simonian's "Lernaganner", "Mountaineer", book.

And now, on the thirtieth anniversary of Simon Simonian's death, the above is my bouquet of words emanating from the heart of his junior compatriot.

Levon Sharoyan
Aleppo, Syria

An Ourish Er…
He Was Different…

"Bédo was my mother's first husband and my father's bosom friend. My father and Bédo had worked together in the same mill. After Bédo's death, my father married his wife, that is to say, my mother.

After his death, Bédo has continued living in our house and continues to live as a husband, as a father and as a friend, but as a foe of a friend. My father, who had loved him as a brother, is the only one who is discontented with Bédo coming back to life. His animosity started after Bédo's interment.

Simonian's mother Ménnoush and her first husband Bédo

I remember well, during my childhood, every time there was bad feeling between my mother and my father, the person responsible for the trouble was Bédo who worked in mysterious ways after his death much like all the great souls, saints and heroes do after their deaths.

Bédo was not a saint or a hero. He was a mere Sassountsi from the Dalvoreeg village. He was the son of an ironsmith. His father had worked in the Dalvoreeg mines extracting iron from the rock veins and melting it to make plows, hatchets, shovels, pickaxes, and rifles. The guns were muzzle type with which he, his brothers and the villagers had defended themselves against attacks by Kurds and Turks. The leaders of the Armenians were Mourad (Hampartsoum Boyadjian), Mihran Damadian, "Baron" Vahan, Kevork Chavoush and other luminaries of the time. It is in honor of Bédo's father and his comrades that the once popular patriotic song, "I am a Brave Son of Dalvoreeg", was sung.

At twenty Bédo had left Sassoun and after working in mills had settled in Aintab much like many Sassountsis. At twenty-five, he had married my mother Ménnoush who was barely eighteen then. Bédo, a handsome, brave young man, had captivated my mother's heart.

"Mother, was Bédo handsome?" I used to ask my mother in my childhood as she recounted stories about him.

"There was no other like him," my mother would say and continue: "He had dark eyebrows and mustache; a handsome posture, a proportioned face. He dressed like a bég. All the girls in our town noted his manly handsomeness. Lucky you, the women would tell me..."

To validate her description, she would open her old chest, the dowry chest, which along with her and much like her, was becoming a worn down witness of old and happy days. From underneath the malodorous, dark blue, apricot and pearl-colored worn out clothes laden with moth, she would pull out her photo bundle, unwrap its silky shroud and hand to me her wedding picture so that I would take a look at Bédo, her Bédo.

My mother's recollection would fill my soul with fascination towards the man who had once been my mother's husband. To further stress so that I would not waiver from the impression I harbored of the dead man, my mother would add: "In this picture, he does not look as handsome as he was. Hey, bygone days. We took this picture in haste. He had just returned from the mill and was covered with flour all over. The neighbors were having their pictures taken. In our days, women did not go to the photographer's shop. We had this picture taken on the spur of that very moment because he refused to change his clothes".

At times, during these mysterious viewing sessions, my father would happen to suddenly step in the house. My mother, with tears still in her eyes, would wrap the picture and place it back. My father, silent and sad, would sit at a corner and inhale the smoke from his cigarette more deeply than usual. My father's sad silence would last for days, sometimes for even weeks during which time he would not speak with my mother.

That absent person beyond the grave thus caused a lot of heartache between my father and my mother. My father's sadness, my mother's tears and the omnipresence of the departed would fill my childhood soul with an unexplainable mystery.

During winter, whenever my father would be absent for months on end working in the mills, my mother would sit around the oven area during the evenings and tell us about Bédo who had told her father "let your 'yes' not be a 'no'". After long deliberation, her father had consented to give his daughter away in marriage to Bédo. After their engagement, during which they had seen each other only once, seven years of blissful marriage followed.

"He was an out of the ordinary man", my mother would tell us; "whenever he missed home, whether there was snow or blizzard, he would walk for four hours in the cold of the night just to come home."

Of course, my mother was the repository of his joy. They thus lived happily but without a child. My mother had believed that on the seventh year of their marriage, she would conceive and carry his child. The seventh year brought with it the unexpected, Bédo's sudden death in the mill during work. There is no need to visualize my mother's torment and agony. My mother would recount his elaborate funeral procession and the overwhelming sadness among the Sassountsis and would particularly emphasize my father's inconsolable lament over the loss of his bosom friend.

Time did not heal my mother's wounds. There had remained only one thing for my mother, visiting her husband's gravesite even in the dead of the winter.

"I remember well," my mother would say. "It was Vartanants Day and I needed to visit his grave at any cost. Our cemetery did not have walls or guards. There was the fear of wolves. My mother was with me. As I was walking among the graves, suddenly Bédo appeared in front of me in the same dress we had him dressed for his interment. I froze. He looked at me and said, 'return home and do not come here anymore'. My mother arrived and saw me standing still. I told her nothing about the occurrence. I grabbed her arm and we returned home. We had not reached Bédo's grave yet. My mother remained perplexed."

That day became a turning point for my mother. From there on she found refuge in her needlework. From a whole year's labor she raised enough funds to place a tombstone on Bédo's grave, on which she had inscribed:

Here Rests Bédo Donoyan
From Dalvoreeg Village, Hagmag Neighborhood
Born 1880, Eternal Rest 1912

However, the thick tombstone with all its weight has not been able to contain Bédo's heart that continues to live on this earth, that is to say, in my mother's heart.

A year passed. My father proposed to marry her. They got married. They started having children. My mother devoted herself to raising her children. But she never forgot her Bédo. The passing years and responsibilities crystallized Bédo's love like a diamond that my mother keeps in her heart. In fact, it's the only crystal she carries in her heart. She raised her children in memory of Bédo. My mother is convinced that we are Bédo's children for, as a matter of fact, Bédo had appeared to her the day before her conception. Without the apparition of Bédo, she claimed, she had never conceived. That is to say, Bédo had become our Holy Ghost!

My mother had willed that when she died she should be buried next to Bédo. However, her exile put an end to that vow. But my mother had taken another solemn vow that neither exile nor war or anything earthly would deter her from that solemn vow. In the afterlife, she would be with her Bédo. My father knew about my mother's alarming preference. That is why he remained melancholic the rest of his life. He knew that there was a fateful separation in store for him in the afterlife.

My mother's preference had me ponder. I have thought that her first love, Bédo's handsomeness and bravery, the loss of her youthful happiness influenced her decision to make her preference known to us. But there was something different with my mother. Whenever I quizzed her, she would only say: "He was different."

My mother admits that my father, her second husband, has been virtuous, God-fearing, good natured, just and has always treated her kindly. But all my father's virtues have given way to the appeal of the deceased. My mother, in her essence, remains the spouse of the deceased. My father carries a wound that never healed because of my mother's total devotion to Bédo. That is why his once bosom friend Bédo, has become his foe after his death for whom he can do no harm with his living self. The other, on the other hand, from the beyond, continues to aggravate my father on Earth.

We, the children, presented alternating stands towards our two fathers. In our childhood, through my mother's tales, we deeply loved Bédo. When we grew older and realized our father's pain, we sided with him and pounded Bédo, who through his interference from the world beyond, caused so much grief to our father. Our assault for a while bore fruits. Bédo's downfall started. But we could never dethrone him for my mother continued to open her wooden chest, unwrap the bundle and with her fingers caress the pictures while murmuring softly "He was different."

We ended our teens, rounded our twenties and became more mature. We ceased to side with either of my parents. It was the period of our neutrality. We let our mother receive her extraterrestrial visitor in our home and continue her affair with him. But we did not let her verbalize her preference to us.

There remains the last chapter for us that will start in the afterlife. We are sure that a separation will take place, our mother will rejoin with her Bédo who is surely waiting impatiently for her. We will remain with our father. Separated from us, our mother will miss us. She will vacillate between her Bédo and us. She will want to join us with Bédo in a threesome arrangement of sorts. My father who despised the Francophone triangle and the ghostly presence of Bédo will not want to have his erstwhile friend turn his foe in our midst. We, who were not accustomed to such things on Earth, will reject our mother's proposition. With each passing day, our mother will miss us more and more. She will eventually concede, leave her Bédo behind and join us, and we will have our family anew.

*****

I wrote this piece after a long delay and reader, be mindful that my mother is an old woman as I write about her Bédo. She has heard from my brothers that I write about Sassountsis. She confronted me once and said: "Son, let it not be that you write about Bédo. He was not like Mano or Magar. He was different."

Forgive me mother, for I wrote about your Bédo.

The Author

 Levon Sharoyan is born in Aleppo, Syria in 1967.

He graduated from the National Haigazian School in 1979 and subsequently from Karen Jeppe Jemaran in 1985.

His foray in literature began in Jemaran's literary periodical "Dzeeler", "Sprouts". While still a student he also began contributing to "Armenia" in Buenos Aires, "Harach" in Paris, and "Marmara" in Istanbul meriting the praise and the encouragement of their editors, Bedros Hadjian, Arpig Missakian and Robert Haddejian respectively. He continues contributing literary reviews and analysis to Armenian Diaspora literary journals and has become a much sought and liked authoritative figure.

Levon has edited and prepared for publication the historically valuable Teotik's fifteen yearbooks (1907-1925). The Calouste Gulbenkian Foundation sponsored their publication from 2006 and onward.

He has published four books "Haverjoren Sireli 'Merin Bolise' ", "The Ever Endearing 'Our Istanbul' "; "Buenos

Aires, Armenia Poghots", "Buenos Aires, Armenia Street"; "Tekeroumner Hai Kiri Yev Badmoutian Kedezrin", "Wandering Along the Shore of Armenian Letters and History"; "Lernagannerou Verchin Sharavighue, Simon Simonian", "The Last Scion of the Mountaineers, Simon Simonian".

He has a number of manuscripts ready for publication that have not seen the light of day due to the civil war in Syria. Among these is one that is devoted to Patriarch Ormanian; and another is titled "Hai Kiri Darontsi 100 Sbasargouner", "100 Servants of Armenian Letters from Daron"

Since 2000, Levon has been a lecturer at the Hamazkayin Institute for Armenian Studies. He has been invited to give lectures in Syria and in other countries about Armenian literature, a subject that remains dear to him.

Levon Sharoyan lives in Aleppo with his wife and two daughters.

His email address is sharoyanlevon@gmail.com.

The Translation Team

Translator: Vahe H. Apelian Ph.D.
                                (Loveland, OH)

Editor: Jack Chelebian, M.D.
                                (Padre Island, TX)

Reviewer: Maria-Eleni Simonian
                                (Huddersfield, England)

Proof reader: Sassoun Simonian
                                (Antelias, Lebanon)

Sponsor: Simon Simonian Fund

Publisher: Hrach Kalsahakian
                                (Dubai, UAE)

Biographical Sketches

Vahe H. Apelian, Ph.D.

Vahe is a retired pharmaceutical scientist. He is the author of a three-volume sequel titled "The Way We Were – The Way We Are". He resides with his wife in Loveland, OH, in the United States of America.

Jack Chelebian, M.D.

Jack is a practicing psychiatrist in Corpus Christi, Texas. He has translated his father's book to English, titled "Dro, Armenia's First Defense Minister". He resides with his wife in Padre Island, Texas, in the United States of America.

Maria-Eleni Simonian

Maria-Eleni is a pharmacy student. In her free time, she writes poems and short stories in both English and Greek. She resides in Huddersfield, West Yorkshire, England.

Sassoun Simonian

Sassoun Holds a B.A. degree in Business Administration and is a Certified Gemologist. He has been devoting his time in organizing his father's, Simon Simonian's archives. He resides in Antelias, Lebanon.

Hrach Kalsahakian

Hrach holds a Masters degree in Human Resources Management. He has translated three books from Armenian to Arabic. He is the founder and the editor of the Middle East Armenian Portal Azad-Hye. He resides with his family in the United Arab Emirates.

58769523R00079